The Price Of Being Kept
A Journey That's Worth it

M. Amber Price

The Price Of Being Kept

Copyright © 2018 M.Amber Price

All rights reserved.

Illustrated by Larry Springfield Jr.

Designed by Helen Price

ISBN:**1986104672**
ISBN-13: **978-1986104678**

Dedication lyrics from the song I Sing Praises To Your Name by Terry MacAlmon

DEDICATION

To my Father God! I give you all the glory, honor, and praise! You have been there for me though it all!

I sing praises to Your name, O Lord,

Praises to Your name, O Lord,

For Your name is great and greatly to be praised!

The Price Of Being Kept

CONTENTS

Acknowledgments   VII

Being Kept	9		
What To Do When Seemingly Nothing is Happening To You	17		
No One Needs To Understand Your Journey	19	Ready	53
Much Better Days Are Ahead	21	Attachments	57
You Are Not Through	27	Know Who You Are	61
You're Not Strange	31	You Are Cared For	65
Keep Your Mind Strong	33	Dealing With Stress	67
Forgiveness Heals You	37	Bold Asking	69
All About Consistency	41	Count It All Joy	73
Where Did The Time Go ?	45	Forever and A Day	75
Stay Above The Storm	49		

The Price Of Being Kept

ACKNOWLEDGMENTS

I want to thank:

My Lord God ! You are my Everything! Many Praises to You!

My Mommy for praying for me and reminding me to focus on the path God has for me.

My Daddy for his support and fun dance breaks to Jackie Wilson.

My sister Joy for making me laugh non stop during this process but yet bothering me the entire time lol.

All of my sisters and brothers. Lisa, Joy, Rodney, Anthony, Lil Joe, Vincent & Don ! I love you all! :-)

My Beautiful Grandma for her great prayers.

All of my Aunties and Uncles for their prayers.

My GodMothers for their prayers.

Memphis Covenant Faith Church.

My Nieces and Nephews. My great Nieces and Nephews.

Watts, California where I was raised.

St. Louis, Missouri, My second home.

New Orleans, Louisiana, My tropical/ Southern/ Parisian place for relaxation.

Dark Chocolate.

Espresso.

Chamomile Tea.

The Price Of Being Kept

1

Being Kept

From a young age, I always heard my mom say, God will keep you if you ask Him to. She often told me the story of how her grandmother taught her about being kept by God. My great-grandmother got a jar, showed it to my mom, and asked her what would happen if the seal was to be broken. My mom replied, " It would get rotten". My mom really knew this because if she didn't close a jar right it would get brown and molded. In that same way, my great-grandmother said God will seal you and keep you if you want Him to. By keeping the bad things from the devil and the world out. Although I've been told that story many times it always fascinates me.

I was still very young, but I loved the sound of being sealed and kept by God. As I grew up that story stayed with me. It wasn't until towards the end of my teens that I fully understood and finally said those words. KEEP ME, LORD I WANT TO BE KEPT. Being kept by the Lord is a wonderful process and I love it, but a lot comes with it. The definition of to keep is to watch over, defend, and to take care of. After I asked God to keep me, I started noticing changes immediately.

There's a confidence that comes from being kept, like God Himself is surrounding you, guarding you and your heart. The glamour of this is you know that no matter what you go through God will be with you. Now the still great, but less popular is the flesh part of you. Even when you try to tiptoe into something bad he swoops you back up (Well, I did ask to be kept huh? Lol). It's like when your mom or dad sees you reaching for the hot stove as a child and then pulling you back from doing so, of course, you cry but it was for your own good.

One of the methods God uses to keep you is what I have learned to call the " stand in " method. A stand-in is someone He sends into your life that you think is permanent, but is really a stand-in for His plans of keeping you. Basically, sending an undercover bodyguard in your life. The part you might get frustrated with is by some chance you become attached to the stand in, then... BOOM! God swoops you back up, but then again, it's for your own good.

After going through, a "God stand-in method", it can cause hurt, but oh how He comes immediately and helps strengthen you back up. Finally, when all is healed you will be like a seasoned cast iron skillet. You now have stronger layers and your ability to cook (love) just gets better.

When you're kept by God and you're not out there doing anything and everything, that is not smoking or drinking or cussing etc., the devil often sends his internal forces to get at you. That's because he knows he can't get you any other way. To me, physical trials could be easier than an internal trial. You can leave a club or a chocolate cake, but you live with your mind 24/7 even when no ones around. That's when worries, anxiety, depression, overthinking, and much more can get at you. You might say if it was a cupcake, I could have just thrown it out. You can't just throw your mind away.

During those personal trials is where if you resist them, you will become much stronger. You must go to God for all your problems and when I say all, I mean all! Even if you have a hangnail. You hear me lol. Yes, God even cares about hangnails, you're His child, of course, He cares about all of you. In order to overcome personal trials, it's a must to keep an open tell all relationship with

God. He wants to help you. You think He wants the devil attacking His child? Absolutely Not! It's our job to rebuke the devil from us. So give it to God, trust, have faith and express what you want Him to take away from you and God will handle it for you!

Holy Reflection Moment

Write about all the negative things you want God to help take away from you.

Physical or Internal.

Tip: For the real personal things just think about them, then ask God to take them from you.

Holy Reflection Moment

Write How God has kept you from a certain situation.

The rest of this book will focus on encouragements to help you in different areas in your life while navigating being kept by God.

The Price Of Being Kept

2

What To Do When Seemingly Nothing Is Happening In Your Life

Congrats! You are at your most real condition. Be proud of being and living. You might not be getting any accolades such as promotions, or personal achievements like marriage, children, etc. You're stripped down in life to just you and God for a wonderful purpose. Be sure to not waste this time, choose to make this experience a positive one.

This is where Gods groundwork begins. Yay! Foundation time! No, not that flawless makeup that has your face beat. I mean a solid structure, like when building a sturdy house. Sure painting and furnishing is quick and beautiful, but what about the excavation process. That is when the digging up of the soil starts (where God digs up the bad in us to deliver us from it). Next comes backfilling and the building of the formwork and much more, then finally the concrete. Even plumbing and electrical later on is intense. Remember a lot goes into building a STRONG home.

The time is now to get all of the uneven stuff in us out before the foundation can be laid. It could be generational clutter, the getting bullied as a child, emotional eating, the heartbreak clutter. Garbage day is today, take all that clutter out and leave it! When we give God our clutter, He won't even leave the smell of stank behind, that's how much He loves us.

Now here's a heads up. Every time you try to let something go, the devil will influence you to bring it back. This is where you fight for your life, yes, it's that serious. Putting God first and meditating on His word day and night is just what it takes to knock that influence out. When God's word keeps coming in, trust that it will knock the evil out. Start by listening to five-minute sermons. Little steps at first. Just read a bible verse a day. Something to help your body, mind, and spirit. Reading the word will energize you and have you singing praise songs to the Lord all day with a gleaming smile because God is so good.

3

No One Needs To Understand Your Journey

You are a wonder to many. You must know that God has a different plan for everyone. If we were all the same there wouldn't be anyone that stood out. Someone might graduate in four years and some in seven. There are those who get married at 22 and some at 48. God has a specific timeline for all of us. It's all about trusting the process every step of the way.

Enjoying your journey is the absolute key. We have to train ourselves not to look to the left or the right but up to God. Focusing on others will just take our eyes off our own blessings. To me, it's much like the growth of a Bamboo tree, as opposed to the Empress tree that grows 30 cm in just three weeks.

Once the Bamboo tree is planted, its growth basically stays underground. Even when being watered it takes five or more years for it to even break ground. Which resembles how God waters us with His word. Where we are growing, but just not where others can see or understand.

Finally one day after years of watering and waiting, you see a little bulb break through the ground. Then what took years to show, amazingly grows 2 feet per day. In just 6 weeks the Bamboo tree grows to be over 90 feet tall! So don't worry about the little plants that grow in a few weeks. You're a God-anointed Bamboo tree whom He has rooted and grounded to make sure you are ready. Once you break ground, everyone will soon see His works in your life whether they are understood or not.

4

Much Better Days Are Ahead

We often tend to hold onto memories too tightly. Now there isn't anything wrong with doing so, but the key is to not hold them captive. Let me explain to you what I mean. Holding good memories captive can distort how you view your future. It can cause discouragement by you thinking that no more good will happen. It also can make you feel that all you needed were those good times and now you're comfortable with just those past accomplishments. But no, it ought not to be so.

Some might think, I wish I was ten years old again, with no worries or responsibilities. Think about it, if you were ten again, you wouldn't even be able to drive or go where you wanted to go or do a multiple of other things. Glamorizing past good times stunt the thankfulness of where you are now.

To me, it's like everyone saying the 90's were the best (which they were & still are lol) or any other decade is best. Instead, we need to try to make this decade the most lit. There were killings and many sad times back then too, people just pushed through. I want you to still enjoy past memories, just don't let them stunt the great memories that God has ahead of you.

Holy Reflection Moment

Write how many negative and angry thoughts you have that were caused from the past that you are still dealing with now.

Aim to lessen them every day. Track the original amount to see your progress.

Holy Reflection Moment

Why do you love God so much? Thankful reflection moment.

Holy Reflection Moment

Write down what you have accomplished today whether big or small.

Even if you just combed your hair today or did laundry etc.

The Price Of Being Kept

5

You Are Not Through

You are filled with so many gifts and talents from God, even some you don't even know about yet. God knows your potential and what you have inside. That's what makes you great. Never let someone tell you that you can't be great in multiple areas. Especially when it says in Philippians 4: 13 NKJV I can do all things through Christ who strengthens me. The gifts that you are suppressing could mean multiple streams of income in your life.

Know how to cook? Write a cookbook or teach cooking classes. Know how to sew? Offer tailoring services. There is never an oversaturated business when God's in it. There could be a million of the same businesses and God will still cause yours to flourish because He has anointed you for it. Not one human being is one dimensional.

For example a woman, yes she's a woman but she can be a daughter, wife, mother, grandmother, granddaughter, niece, cousin, or friend. Yet she is still herself. Being multifaceted and multi-talented could be one in the same. Be the chef, author, shoemaker the list can go on and on. God has made us all the best in every capacity. He has built in us a never-ending well of purpose. Today tap into your known and unknown talents. Ask God to lead and guide you. Remember before you start anything to make sure to go to God first. It says in Proverbs 16: 3 Commit (give) to the LORD whatever you do, and He will establish your plans. So give God your plans. Trust Him and He will see you through.

Holy Reflection Moment

Write Something you've always wanted to pursue.

The Price Of Being Kept

6

You Are Not Strange

No one else is you. They don't know what you go through on the daily. One thing people really don't know is when God gives you discernment. Whether it's toward a broad situation or a specific person. For instance, God might give you discernment about someone that everyone still sees in a good light. It's now up to you to walk in the spirit while having the knowledge of what God has revealed about that person.

Now if you have told anyone and they haven't received that knowledge then now you're seen as strange. You know the term ignorance is bliss. Well once knowledge is revealed it's time to be responsible. It's your responsibility to know that not everyone will understand the wisdom God has given you. Whenever God gives you personal wisdom it's not always easy to handle.

Here are some steps to take. First, ask God to help you handle that knowledge. Next, pray for whoever He has given you discernment about. Then, be strong because it can be frustrating when you're seen as acting strange when you're just walking in the spirit. It says in John 14: 17 The Spirit will show you what is true. The people of this world cannot accept the Spirit, because they don't see or know him. But you know the Spirit, who is with you and will keep on living in you. So forgive those who call you strange for they do not know. Just keep them in your prayers. Remember Godly wisdom is a gift and you are never strange to God. You are highly looked upon by God. He definitely understands you completely.

7

Keep Your Mind Strong

Fight the devil from off your mind. I know I've mentioned this in a previous chapter but I want to expand on it. The mind is where basically everything starts. We must keep a leash on our thinking. Everything could be perfect, then all of a sudden you get a crazy thought. People can either act on that crazy thought or rebuke it. What has to be done is to always listen to the word of God.

There was a time where I was slacking in my prayer life. I was so busy and just tired of going through things, but what I really needed to do to control those things was to go to God. God said to me Amber, you diligently serve and clean around the house to help your family, but I want you to diligently seek me to help yourself. It says towards the end of Hebrews 11: 6 that He rewards those who [earnestly and diligently] seek Him. Since I know how great God and His rewards are they just don't consist of material things that money can buy. They consist of mental and physical strength, confidence, and assurance. Even if you think that you're strong and don't need God you still do! Our own self-strength without the supernatural strength God gives us never fully pans out as we might think. As a strong person, it's okay to show emotions. When people know that you're a strong person they don't really check up on you like that. But it can surely build up.

No one is perfect. We aren't robots just void of feeling. If you are usually a strong person but have an emotional moment, it does not make you weak. I repeat, it does NOT make you weak. You are human! If anything, it needed to be let out. Even Jesus cried, which is found in John 11:35. Sometimes a good cry is all you need.

Tears to me are just mind, soul and spirit sweat from the exercise of emotional battles. Even if you have to let it out by just telling someone you trust what is going on. The devil doesn't want you to let it out or tell anyone because he wants to be the only one that has control of your mind. NO! By letting it out it takes away the chance for it to fester into something worse. Make a choice today to not listen when those negative things come to your mind.

Holy Reflection Moment

Go to a quiet place and take a few moments to have a good cry. Then give all your worries over to God and ask Him to help you with what's going on in your life.

The Price Of Being Kept

8

Forgiveness Heals

Not forgiving others hurts you and your life. It really hurts you more than them. It's not worth it. Basically not forgiving is trying to take control and leave God out of the situation. This really makes matters worse. So we must bring it to God and not only release out love and forgiveness, release out the anger of the specific situation. Say, Lord, it's yours, I give it to you to handle it. When you hold on to anger you lose yourself. Normally your personality is great and outgoing. But by choosing not to forgive, it changes. Then people will notice and see that you're miserable. All the while the person who hurt you is living life normally. Yes I know it's not fair. Yes, I know you're angry and yes what the person did was bad. Life is all about choices. Would what they did even matter to you in a year. If not then release that so you can know yourself again. I know you don't feel like yourself. Make that change. Forgiving is a release. A release of rage, hurt, and disrupted peace. What is gained from not forgiving? Think about it. Absolutely nothing. Sometimes it's easier for some people to hold grudges forever instead of apologizing or letting go. If you don't watch out you will become accustomed to the pride of having a beef. Like " yea I have a beef with everybody". That's not something to be proud of. Of course, not everyone will like you, but that's their problem. Let it only be a one-sided situation. It may be hard but keep your heart right, God will deal with their hearts.

Everyone doesn't have to like you. Not everyone liked Jesus and still don't. If they did it to the green tree they will surely do it to the brown tree. Meaning if they hated on Jesus who is perfect in every way possible, it's a given you will be hated on. Why does it bother us so much when people don't like us? It really shouldn't be a big deal. What does them not liking us have anything to do with us. Nothing! So for your own personal peace forgive those who don't like you for whatever the reason. Know that you are very liked and well loved by God.

Holy Reflection Moment

Think about who you need to forgive in order to help your personal peace.

The Price Of Being Kept

9

All About Consistency

Life is about consistency. Yes, you are being kept by God, but we must put in some work too. Exercising, eating right, and reading Gods word are all good, but they won't make a difference unless we are consistent. Consistency shows up in simple everyday areas. You could be on snapchat taking a picture that's not looking how you want it to. Do you just stop? No, you choose another filter and change your angle to get the picture you want. I myself have had a problem with consistency. Every year, I buy new yarn and prepare to make something. Well, I start with the best intentions of finishing, but it never comes together. A lot of great things could be accomplished if only we had of stayed consistent.

My remedy for lack of consistency is to go to God. You might say " go to God again?" Yes, always go to God. Pray that God may give you the grace to be consistent in all things. When God graces you for it, it's like being held accountable spiritually. So, even if you don't feel like it, the grace and energy for it will spring up from inside of you to do what you have to do at the appointed time.

It's okay not to be perfect, no one is. Just try and consistency will come. Consistency is an act of faith. Faith that what you are doing will pay off. In the Bible, Peter had the faith to walk on the water towards Jesus. It was just the lack of consistent faith that caused him to start to drown. The great thing about Jesus was in Matthew 14: 31. Immediately Jesus reached out his hand and caught him. That means that even though Peter fell, Jesus honored his act of trying and helped him. Immediately Jesus reached out his hand that means he had made it close enough for Jesus to help him. It's a must for us to get and stay close enough to God, so even if we do fall, He sees us trying and helps us. Consistency is key. God is such a good God. He will notice and reward your consistency!

Personal Reflection Moment

Write a few things that you need to start being consistent about.

The Price Of Being Kept

10

Where Did the Time Go?

Weren't we all just considered kids like 2 seconds ago? It's like our whole lives we were told we weren't old enough for this or that. Just living our lives carefree while wanting to be older and do more stuff. Then one day you're in your 20s not knowing what to do with your life. I really think the transition to adulthood needs to be better. For me personally, I feel as though children and teenagers aren't being prepared like they need to be.

Yes, there are those who just have it all together. Then there are those who have to deal with mental personal stress, financial problems, or have older parents who just didn't push them to do certain things. We all know the saying "you can't blame anyone but yourself." I say you don't need to blame others or yourself. Growing up involves some growing pains. We now have to think about careers, marriage, children and so much more. I want to tell you that it's okay not to know what to do. We must go to God and trust Him to lead and guide us for a life that we've never even lived before.

It's important not to think about what others might think about your life. No one is you, they don't know how you have had to fight just to even get to where you are now. People might look down on you for not going to college or not having a job or having a child. The person might not have the money to go to college or they may not get accepted into the college of their choice. They don't have a job? Hire them then. Also, some women have fertility issues. The world needs to stop judging and applying pressure to people.

Yes, it is great to succeed but if a person is taking longer to do so don't shun them. Know that God loves you and is proud of you no matter what you do. In Jeremiah 29:11 it says For I know the plans I have for you," declares the LORD, "plans to prosper you and not to harm you, plans to give you hope and a future." God has great plans for you. Block out all of the negative and judging of others. Stay focused on Him and everything will be just fine.

Holy Reflection Moment

Breathe. It is not too late to accomplish everything that you desire. Think of the things that are good. Just live your best life and don't go back and forth with.. anybody!!

The Price Of Being Kept

11

Stay Above The Storm

In life, storms come. When they do I want to provide an alternative to the usual worry. God! God has and always will be our peace in the middle of the storm. God has worked through the eagle to be an example of how to have peace through storms. All the other birds seek shelter during storms but the eagle isn't fazed by the storm. Eagles fly above the storm while using the roaring winds to accelerate their wings to fly higher. That's a word lol. We must use the storms that we go through as motivation for escalation.

Storms are hard but it's in the storms, that if we will be still and go above them, God will help us the most. I know for a fact that God is an ever-present help. Whether it's financial or emotional or any type of troubled storm He will keep you. You must keep an elevated mindset to keep your mind above the storm. It's easy to be like yea I'm above it, then you get by yourself in your room and negative thoughts fill your mind. An elevated mindset can be needed during rain or shine. Troubles don't last always, but thoughts of them might linger. So refuse to let bad times rule you. God will help you rule over them.

Reflection moment

Try to think back on a time God helped you get through a storm. Give Him some thanks!

The Price Of Being Kept

12

Ready

God will prepare you for success, but first He makes sure that you are ready. He has to know that you can handle the upgrades without them destroying you. Only God knows when you are ready. God's plan isn't something you can rush. Trust me I have tried many times lol. You can't! But you do feel when you're almost ready though. It's an inward downloading into the spirit that God gives you. Like you're ready for everything. Feeling like you have been spiritually and mentally prepared.

The feeling where you know in faith, with of course the help of the Lord, you are indeed ready. In the dictionary, there are a few different meanings of ready. Ready means to be keen or quick to give, eager, inclined, ready to do something, and to prepare (someone or something) for an activity or purpose. Being ready is God's time to show himself through you. Oh, what a time it will be. Ephesians 3:20 says, Now to Him who is able to do immeasurably more than all we ask or imagine, according to his power that is at work within us, NIV. What God has gotten you ready for, you can't even imagine how great it will be. So take your time and remember that God is readying you. Say "His time not mine". Choose to trust in God's timing and I pray that you will receive all that is being made ready for you in the name of Jesus.

Holy Reflection Moment

What do you think you are ready for?

Holy Reflection Moment

What does God have to work out in you

& deliver you from, for you to be ready?

13

Attachments

When we have good times with people or with things like video games or television it could lead to becoming attached to those things. Now there isn't anything wrong with being attached to people, but we must do so being attached to God first. My mom has always said you can tell when a child is well loved because they are not out running to everyone for affection. They get enough love from their parents. In that same way, we get more than enough love from our Daddy God.

Remember His side of love isn't the problem, it's ours. We must believe and receive His love for it to take effect so that we will want to be more attached to Him. I love my sister, so when she goes out of town, I maybe miss her lol. We have so many TV shows that we love and watch together as well as movies and favorite foods etc. For me, it's a must to stay close to God so that I won't bother my sis lol. Being attached to God helps with your relationship with others so that they don't have to share every moment with you and you will still be fine.

Now when she came back, I had so many funny memes to show her and so many tv episodes to watch. But because I stayed close to God, I didn't overcrowd her. So know that it's okay to have fun times with people, tv, and video games. We just need to make sure that we put God first and be attached to Him because with God we will never go unloved. God is a good God. He loves you and wants to be close to you and for you to be more close to Him than you are with anyone else.

Holy Reflection Moment

Think of some things or people that you want to stop being attached to. Get closer to God and watch how you will want to be less attached to them.

The Price Of Being Kept

14

Know Who You Are

To me, the key to knowing fully who you are is to know whose you are. It would be like being apart of the royal family yet thinking of yourself as nothing. As Christians, we are in a much better royal family. Being born into royalty to do great things! In Jeremiah 1:5 it shows us, "Before I formed you in the womb I knew you, before you were born I set you apart; I appointed you as a prophet to the nations." Our Heavenly Father has provided us such a privilege. He died on the cross for our sins and not only that, He took away all sickness and disease, poverty, lack, want, depression and so much more. We must continually believe that He took all of those things from us.

We must receive the royal lifestyle He has set up for His children. God doesn't have any grandchildren only CHILDREN. We are His! Every single one of His children are the apple of His eye. 1 Peter 2:9 says, But you are a chosen people, a royal priesthood, a holy nation, God's special possession, that you may declare the praises of Him who called you out of darkness into His wonderful light. We are in His wonderful light! You have to know how handsome and beautiful you are as well! There have always been certain qualities that the world has magnified. There are also many that have been forced to be seen as never good enough. Genesis 1:27 reads, So God created mankind in his own image, in the image of God he created them; male and female he created them. You must believe and know that no matter what size or skin tone you are, you are beautiful! God made us to look like Him.

If anyone has ever bullied you and called you ugly or any other terrible names they are in trouble! They basically really called God those things. Do you think God appreciates when His creations who look like Him are talked about? Absolutely not. I hope that these words get stuck in your heart and mind. I hope you feel regality in your spirit. Live it! Be it! We are made in God's image!

Holy Reflection Moment

Want to feel royal?

Take a few minutes each day and dip in God's word. Also, make sure to pamper yourself each day. Put your feet up and watch your fav television show for an hour! Exfoliate! Lounge for 30 minutes in your favorite robe. Have the spirit of regality each day.

The Price Of Being Kept

15

You Are Cared For

God cares about you so much. You know how great fathers care for and love their children? Now imagine how our Heavenly Father cares and loves us with an unconditional love. God's main objective is to make us feel special and to constantly show us how much He cares for us. Isaiah 46:4 says "I am your God and will take care of you until you are old and your hair is gray. I made you and will care for you; I will give you help and rescue you." That pretty much said it all! Lol! End of chapter.

We as His children might not be perfect, but that still never stops Him from caring. Ephesians 1: 4-6 shows how even before the creation of the world He chose us! " Even as [in His love] He chose us [actually picked us out for Himself as His own] in Christ before the foundation of the world, that we should be holy (consecrated and set apart for Him) and blameless in His sight, even above reproach, before Him in love. 5 For He foreordained us (destined us, planned in love for us) to be adopted (revealed) as His own children through Jesus Christ, in accordance with the purpose of His will. 6 (What pleasure he took in planning this!) He wanted us to enter into the celebration of his lavish gift-giving by the hand of his beloved Son.

So when situations happen know that God cares. Read these scriptures every day to get them in your spirit. You will become more and more confident and know for sure that God cares for you!

16

Dealing With Stress

Stress can be caused by many things, finances, relationships troubles, weight etc. The type of stress I'm going to talk about is another type of stress. The type when you're working and doing things out of the goodness of your heart. You don't mind the work aspect, it's just you rather do something that you like to do. Whether it's toward your degree or getting ahead in your job so you can get a promotion, or even finishing a book that God has placed on your heart. Those are the things you don't mind working toward. It's the taxing things that you feel are not adding any value to your personal life. It's really tough, trust me, I know, but it will all be worth it. James 1 2-4 says, Consider it pure joy, my brothers, and sisters, whenever you face trials of many kinds because you know that the testing of your faith produces perseverance. Let perseverance finish its work so that you may be mature and complete, not lacking anything.

We've all heard of the quote " Do what you have to do, so you can do what you want to do." I say do what you do for others out of the love God gives you for them, and for sure God will make ways for you to have all of the desires of your heart. Anything we do for others is a seed. Seeds that are watered by having a good attitude while doing them. In return, the Lord sees and will bring forth a great harvest from it. Don't get discouraged if the harvest of the seeds you have sown you don't see yet.

There is an episode of Spongebob where his pineapple is gone. As he prepares to move he sheds a tear and unknowingly waters another pineapple seed. So while Squidward is rejoicing (the devil and negative people). The seed is preparing to grow. Sometimes you have to give it just a few more minutes. Just as Patrick was trying to stop the car taking up more time, BOOM another fresh new pineapple house grew in the old one's place! Even on top of Squidward! So don't get discouraged when you don't see things coming to pass. No more stressing! God is simultaneously working things out for your good!

17

Bold Asking

The definition of bold is a confident and courageous way; showing a willingness to take risks. How we approach our Father God is always with respect. Yet when we have a personal relationship with Him, we have the confidence to ask boldly of the things we desire from Him. I personally would be irritated if someone asked me for some water in a timid afraid way. Like, just ask already. Come boldly to me and simply ask. James 1:5 says If you don't know what you're doing, pray to the Father. He loves to help. You'll get his help, and won't be condescended to when you ask for it. Ask boldly, believingly, without a second thought.

God wants us to have our hearts desires. Some might say, well He already knows what I need so why should I ask. An example could be a fast food restaurant. They know that you are hungry, but unless you ask for exactly what you want they can not give it to you. God knows what you need, healing, prosperity, a God-given mate. Just ask Him for what you want and be specific! Nothing shows God that you have confidence in Him more than asking boldly of Him! So let's always respect His position, honoring His great authority and power, yet come boldly as His children, because He loves us very much.

Holy Reflection Moment

Ask God boldly and specifically of what you want today! He loves and cares for us and He will give it to you if you believe.

The Price Of Being Kept

18

Count It All Joy

It says in Romans 15:13 May the God of your hope so fill you with all joy and peace in believing [through the experience of your faith] that by the power of the Holy Spirit you may abound *and* be overflowing (bubbling over) with hope. It's important to always hope in the Lord. This next scripture should encourage you :-) 1 Peter 5:10 And after you have suffered a little while, the God of all grace [Who imparts all blessing and favor], Who has called you to His [own] eternal glory in Christ *Jesus*, will Himself complete *and* make you what you ought to be, establish *and* ground you securely, and strengthen, and settle you. So don't try to get out of anything prematurely. So you can become mature and well-developed, not deficient in any way.

Even when things in life aren't going like you want them to, count it all JOY!! When I'm making breakfast and the oatmeal overflows in the microwave, I take a second and pause. Instead of getting frustrated, I count it all joy that I have food to eat. Being grateful for even the most seemingly minuscule things can make joy spring forth in your heart and soul. Having joy is a choice. Choose joy today. Proverbs 15:23 says a person finds joy in giving an apt reply—and how good is a timely word! I pray that this is a timely word for you. May the joy of the Lord be your strength every single day of your life!

19

Forever and a Day

Trouble doesn't last always. God will always be with you forever and a day! 1 John 5:11 says, And this is the testimony: God has given us eternal life, and this life is in His Son. Wonderful eternal life! Gods got you forever and ever! 1 John 5:13 says, I write these things to you who believe in the name of the Son of God so that you may know that you have eternal life. You must believe in the name of Jesus!

Believing will release the wisdom and knowledge that God wants to impart to you. It says in Psalms 9: 7-12 But the LORD abides forever; He has established His throne for judgment, And He will judge the world in righteousness; He will execute judgment for the peoples with equity. The LORD also will be a stronghold for the oppressed, A stronghold in times of trouble; And those who know Your name will put their trust in You, For You, O LORD, have not forsaken those who seek You. Sing praises to the LORD, who dwells in Zion;

Declare among the peoples His deeds. He remembers all of those who suffer; He does not forget the cry of the afflicted".

You are very dearly loved by God. If you just seek Him, you will not be forsaken (abandoned/or left). Our Father God knows, cares, and loves us so much that He never forgets anytime we cry and shed tears. His love is the only one that is unconditional and forever. So always remember you are special to Him. Know that He wants to keep you, so just ask Him to. He LOVES YOU!

I hope that this book has been a blessing to you. Remember that being kept by God isn't easy but it's worth it!

The Price Of Being Kept